PIANO · VOCAL · GUITAR

THE beach boys ANTHOLOGY

CONTENTS

ISBN 978-0-634-03245-5

HAL•LEONARD®
CORPORATION
7777 W. BLUEMOUND RD. P.O. BOX 13819 MILWAUKEE, WI 53213

Visit Hal Leonard Online at
www.halleonard.com

ALL SUMMER LONG

Words and Music by BRIAN WILSON
and MIKE LOVE

CALIFORNIA GIRLS

Words and Music by BRIAN WILSON
and MIKE LOVE

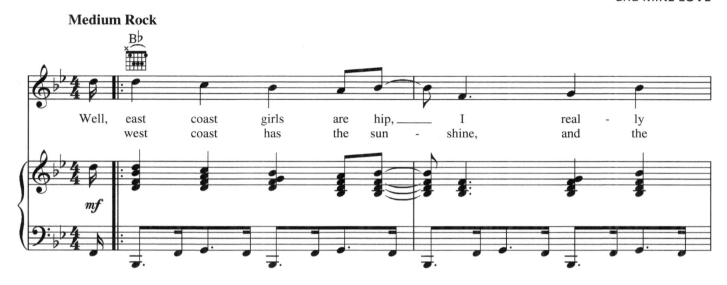

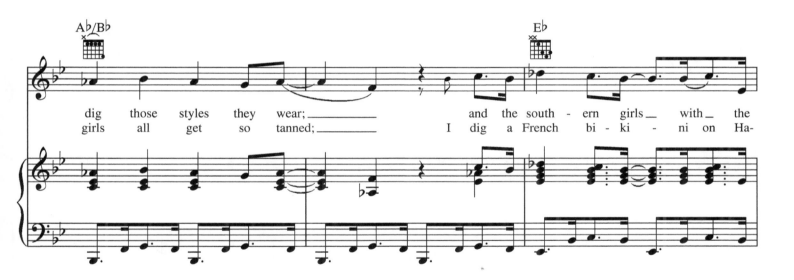

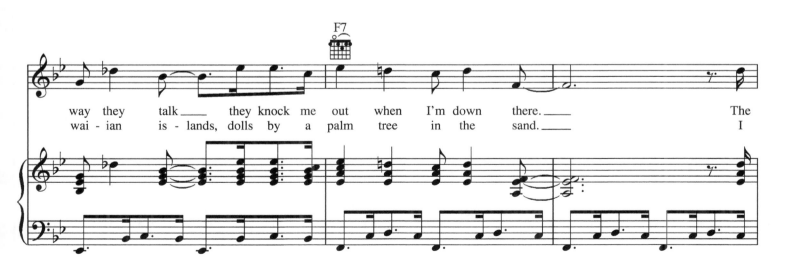

BARBARA ANN

Words and Music by
FRED FASSERT

Bright Rock

(Ba, ba, ba, ba,___ Ba'-'bra Ann. Ba, ba, ba, ba,___ Ba'-'bra Ann) Ba'-'bra

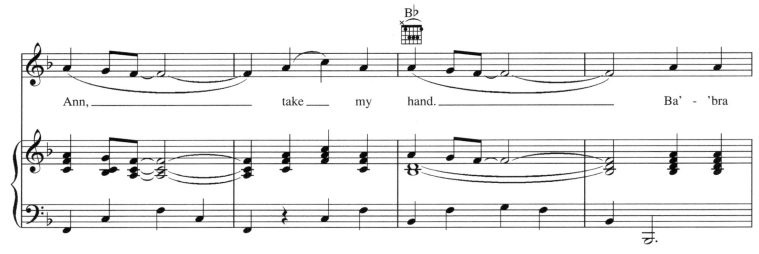

Ann, ___ take ___ my hand. ___ Ba'-'bra

Ann, ___ you got me rock-in' and a-roll-in', rock-

BE TRUE TO YOUR SCHOOL

Words and Music by BRIAN WILSON
and MIKE LOVE

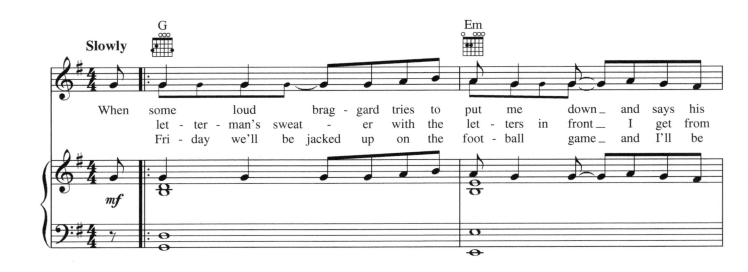

CAROLINE, NO

Words and Music by BRIAN WILSON
and TONY ASHER

Moderately slow

Where did your long hair go? _____

Where is the girl I used to know? _____ How could you

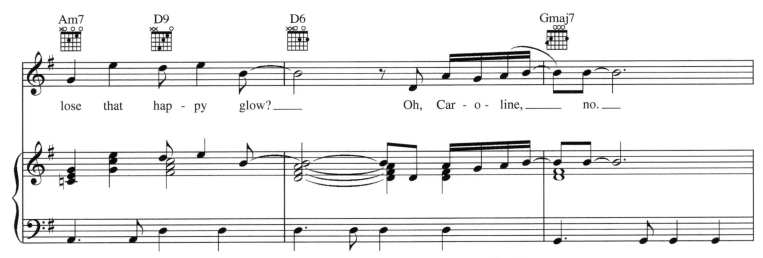

lose that hap-py glow? _____ Oh, Car-o-line, _____ no. _____

Original key: G♭ major. This edition has been transposed up one half-step to be more playable.

Oh Car - o - line, _____ no. _____

CATCH A WAVE

Words and Music by BRIAN WILSON
and MIKE LOVE

Throw me a fa - vor, try the great - est sport a - round.
Not just a fad 'cause it's been go - ing on so long.
So take a les - son from a top notch surf - er boy:

Ev - 'ry - bod - y tries it
All the surf - ers go - ing
ev - 'ry Sat - ur - day,

once. Those who don't just have to put it down.
strong. They said it would - n't last too long.
boy, but don't you treat it like a toy.

DANCE, DANCE, DANCE

Words and Music by BRIAN WILSON,
CARL WILSON and MIKE LOVE

Moderate Rock

After six hours of school __ I've had e-
feel __ put down, __ I try to
week - end dance __ we like to

nough for the day. __ I hit the ra - di - o dial __ and turn it
shake it off quick. __ With my chick by my side, __ the ra - di -
show __ up last. __ I play it cool when it's slow __ and jump

up all the way. __
o does the trick. __ } I got - ta dance __ right on the
it when it's fast. __

DARLIN'

Words and Music by BRIAN WILSON
and MIKE LOVE

You know, if words could say, __
I was liv-ing like half a man; __

that dar-ling I'd find a way __ to let you know what you meant __ to me. ____
then I could-n't love but now I can. __ You pick me up when I'm feel-ing sad, __

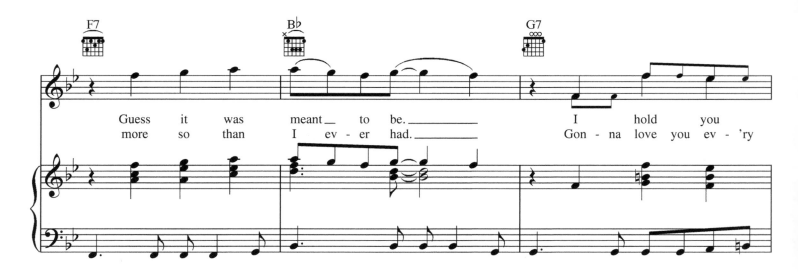

Guess it was meant __ to be. ____ I hold you
more so than I ev-er had. ____ Gon-na love you ev-'ry

DO IT AGAIN

Words and Music by BRIAN WILSON
and MIKE LOVE

With a solid beat

It's au-to-mat-ic when I talk with old friends and

con-ver-sa-tion turns to girls we knew, when their hair was soft and

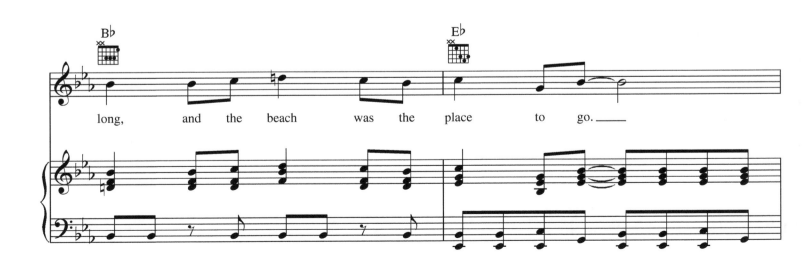

long, and the beach was the place to go. ___

DON'T WORRY BABY

Words and Music by BRIAN WILSON
and ROGER CHRISTIAN

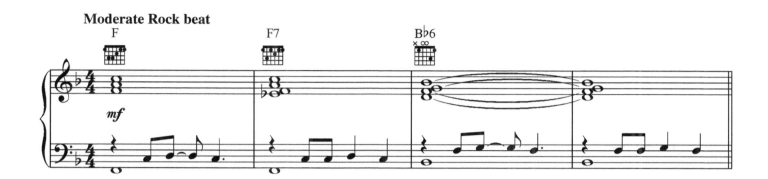

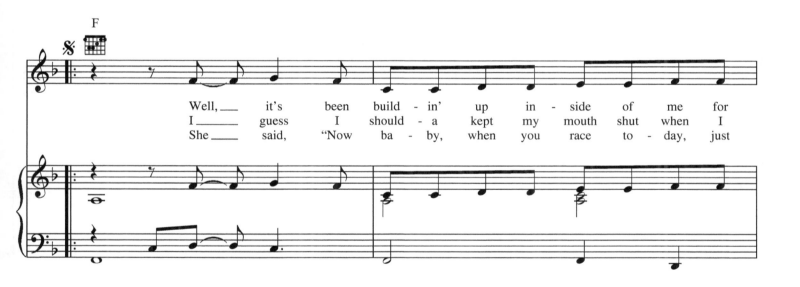

DO YOU WANT TO DANCE?

Words and Music by
BOBBY FREEMAN

DON'T BACK DOWN

Words and Music by BRIAN WILSON
and MIKE LOVE

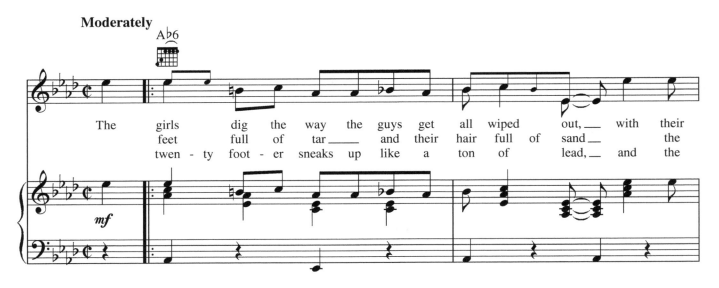

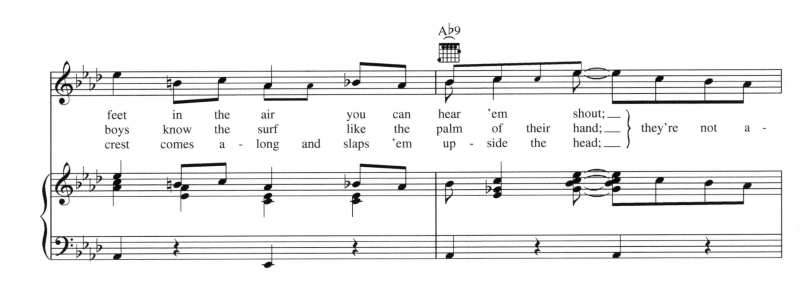

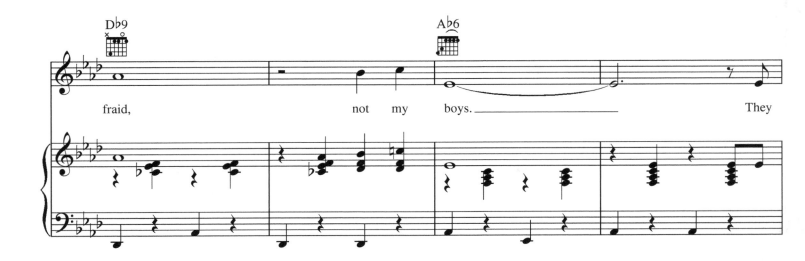

409

Words and Music by BRIAN WILSON,
GARY USHER and MIKE LOVE

Repeat and Fade

GIRLS ON THE BEACH

Words and Music by BRIAN WILSON
and MIKE LOVE

FUN, FUN, FUN

Words and Music by BRIAN WILSON
and MIKE LOVE

GOD ONLY KNOWS

Words and Music by BRIAN WILSON
and TONY ASHER

GOOD VIBRATIONS

Words and Music by BRIAN WILSON
and MIKE LOVE

HELP ME RHONDA

Words and Music by BRIAN WILSON
and MIKE LOVE

HEROES AND VILLAINS

Words and Music by BRIAN WILSON
and VAN DYKE PARKS

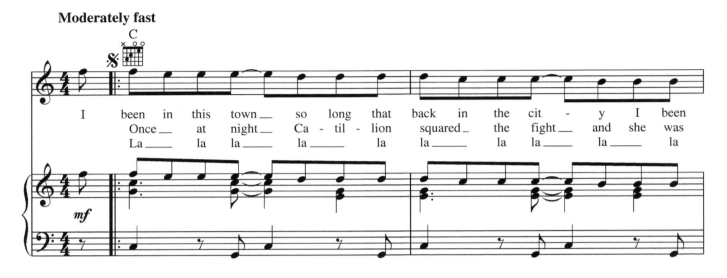

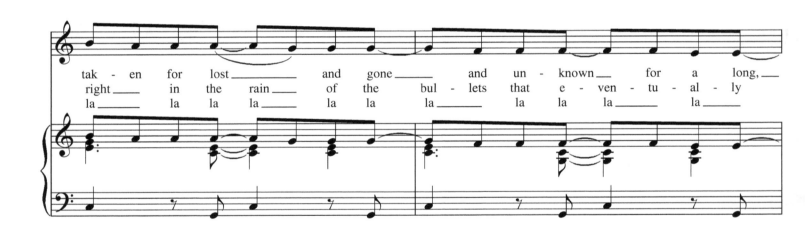

54

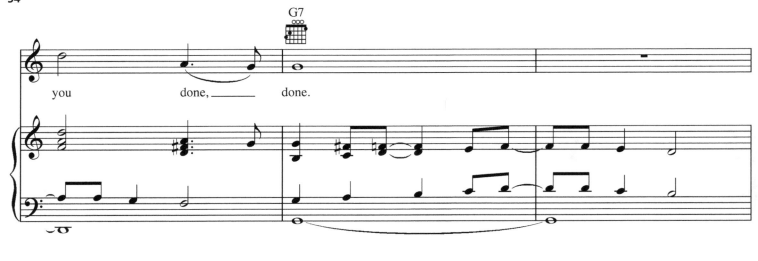

you done, _____ done.

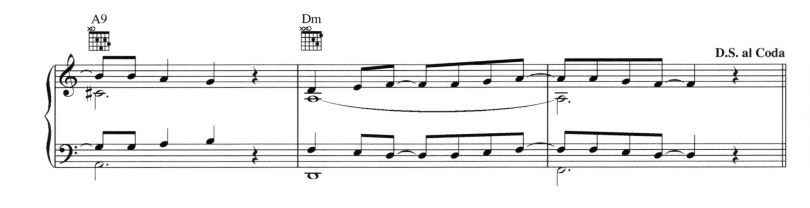

D.S. al Coda

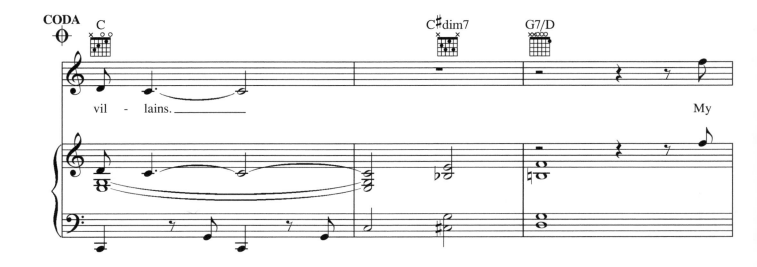

vil - lains. _____

My

I GET AROUND

Words and Music by BRIAN WILSON
and MIKE LOVE

same ol' strip,__ I got-ta find a new place where the kids are hip.__

nev-er been beat__ and__ we've nev-er missed yet with the girls we meet.__

My bud-dies and me__ are get-tin'

None of the guys go stead - y 'cause it

real well-known,__ yeah, the bad guys know us and they leave us a-lone.__ } I get a-

would-n't be right__ to leave your best girl home on a Sat-ur-day night.__

C

A7

round _____ from town to town _____

IN MY ROOM

Words and Music by BRIAN WILSON
and GARY USHER

Moderately slow

There's a room where I can go and
In this world I lock out all my
Now it's dark and I'm a - lone but

tell my se - crets to, }
wor - ries and my cares } in ___ my
I won't be a - fraid,

room, ___ in ___ my

IT'S OK

Words and Music by BRIAN WILSON
and MIKE LOVE

Moderate Rock

Fun is in, it's no sin, it's that time a - gain___ to shed your
good down the hood of a fun - ky ride_____ on the
K to get out there and have some fun___ by your-

load, hit the road, on the run a - gain.___ Sum - mer
way to the tide just to tan your hide.___ In the
self may - be or else just with a spe - cial one.___ Good or

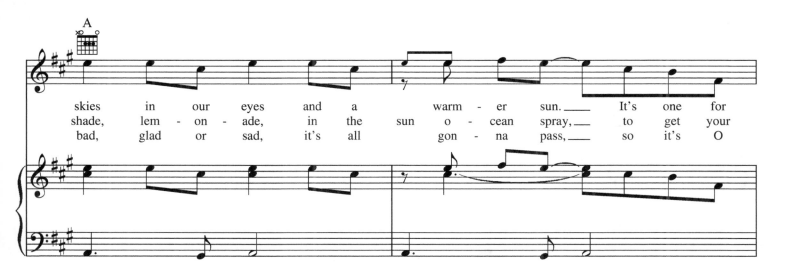

skies in our eyes and a warm - er sun.___ It's one for
shade, lem - on - ade, in the sun o - cean spray,___ to get your
bad, glad or sad, it's all gon - na pass,___ so it's O

KEEP AN EYE ON SUMMER

Words and Music by BRIAN WILSON
and BOB NORBERG

Original key: F♯ major. This edition has been transposed down one half-step to be more playable.

KOKOMO
from the Motion Picture COCKTAIL

Words and Music by MIKE LOVE, TERRY MELCHER,
JOHN PHILLIPS and SCOTT McKENZIE

Moderately bright

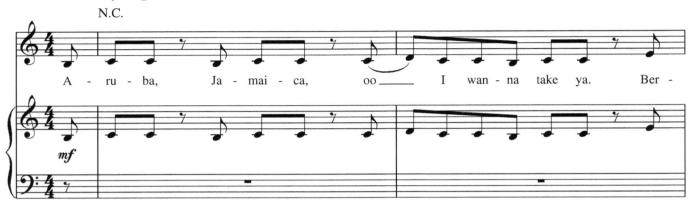

A - ru - ba, Ja - mai - ca, oo___ I wan - na take ya. Ber -

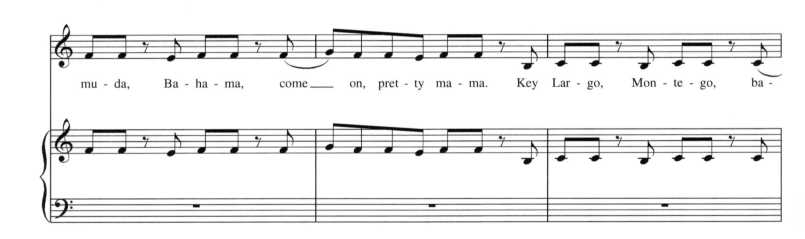

mu - da, Ba - ha - ma, come___ on, pret - ty ma - ma. Key Lar - go, Mon - te - go, ba -

- by, why don't we go, Ja - mai - ca. Off the Flor - i - da Keys___ We'll put out to sea___

LITTLE DEUCE COUPE

Music by BRIAN WILSON
Words by ROGER CHRISTIAN

THE LITTLE GIRL I ONCE KNEW

Words and Music by
BRIAN WILSON

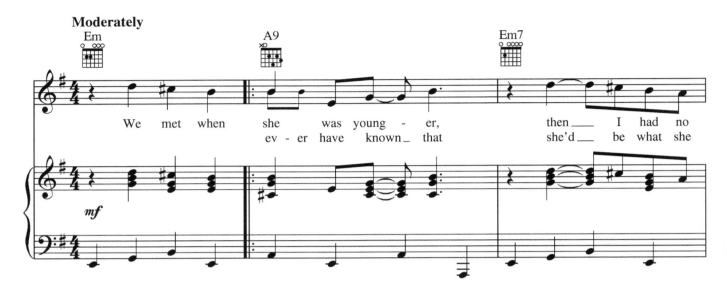

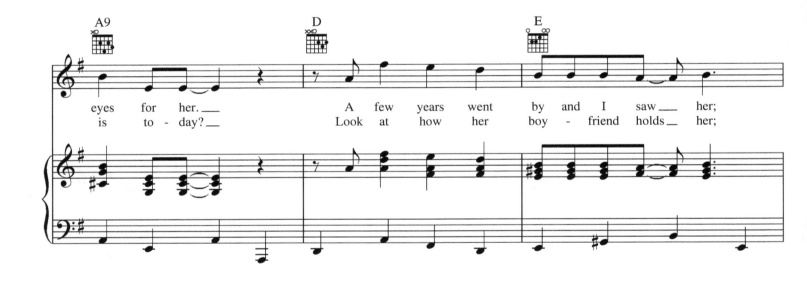

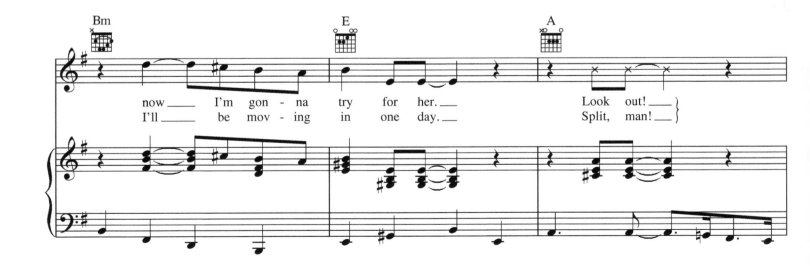

LITTLE HONDA

Words and Music by BRIAN WILSON
and MIKE LOVE

Bright Rock beat

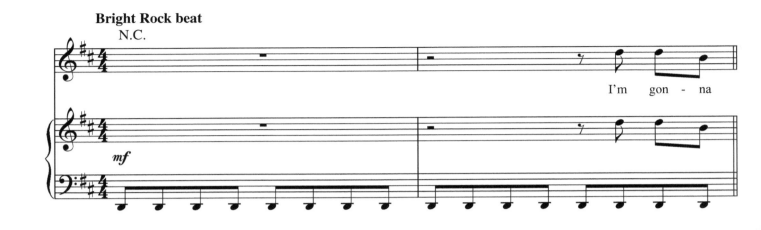

wake you up early 'cause I'm gon - na take a ride with you.
big mo - tor - cy - cle, just a groov - y lit - tle mo - tor - bike.
hills like a match - less 'cause my Hon - da's built real - ly light.

We're go - in' down to the Hon - da shop, I'll
It's more fun than a bar - rel of
When I go in - to the turns lean with

PLEASE LET ME WONDER

Words and Music by BRIAN WILSON
and MIKE LOVE

LITTLE SAINT NICK

Words and Music by BRIAN WILSON
and MIKE LOVE

Original key: G♭ major. This edition has been transposed up one half-step to be more playable.

PET SOUNDS

By BRIAN WILSON

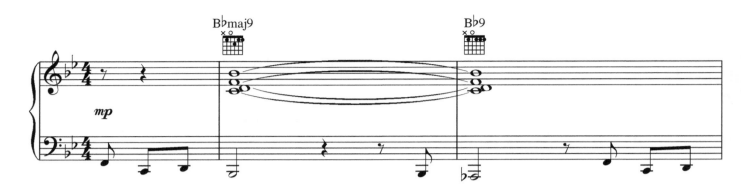

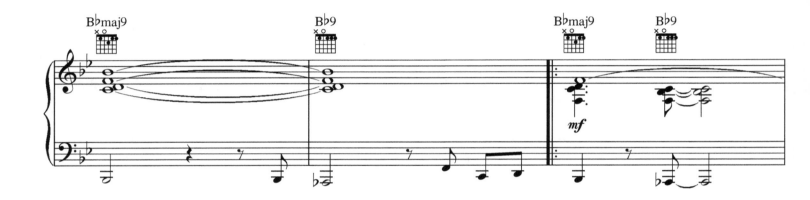

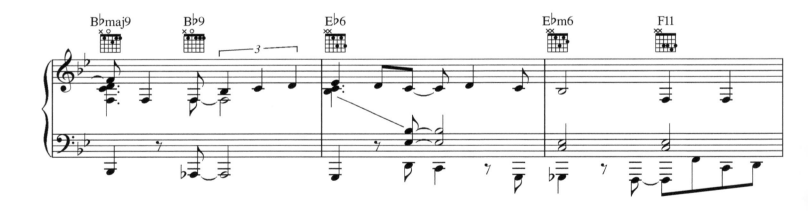

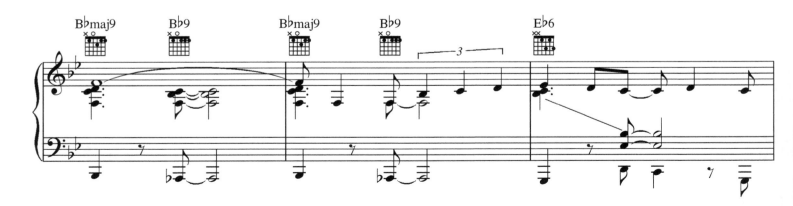

SHUT DOWN

Words by ROGER CHRISTIAN
Music by BRIAN WILSON

Bright Rock beat

Tach it up, tach it up, bud-dy, gon-na shut you down. ___

It hap-pened on the strip where the road is wide, ___
De - clin - in' num - bers at an e - ven rate, ___
Ped - al's to the floor, hear his dual quads drink, ___ and now the

two cool shorts stand - in' side by side. ___ Yeah, my
at the count of one we both ac - cel - er - ate. ___ My
Four thir - teen's lead is start - in' to shrink. ___ He's

SLOOP JOHN B

Words and Music by
BRIAN WILSON

Moderately

We come out in the Sloop John B, my grand - fa - ther and
first mate, he got drunk. He broke in the Cap - tain's
poor cook, he got the fits. He threw a - way all my

me. A - round Nas - sau town we _____ do
trunk. The con - sta - ble had ___ to come and take him a -
grits. Then ___ he took ___ and he ate up all of my

roam, drink - ing all night,
way. Sher - iff John Stone,
corn. Let ___ me go home.

SURFER GIRL

Words and Music by
BRIAN WILSON

SURFER'S RULE

Words and Music by BRIAN WILSON
and MIKE LOVE

It's plas-tered on the wall all a-round the school now, ___
burn it on the grass on the foot-ball __ field now; __
wood-ie ball of surf-ers ball-ing 'long-side the wag-on, __

_____
be-com-ing just as com-mon as the
just try to make them cool it and they'll
the hoe-dad-dies sit-tin' while the

Gold-en Rule now. _____
nev-er yield now. _____
surf-ers are drag-gin'. _____ The

SURFIN'

Words and Music by BRIAN WILSON
and MIKE LOVE

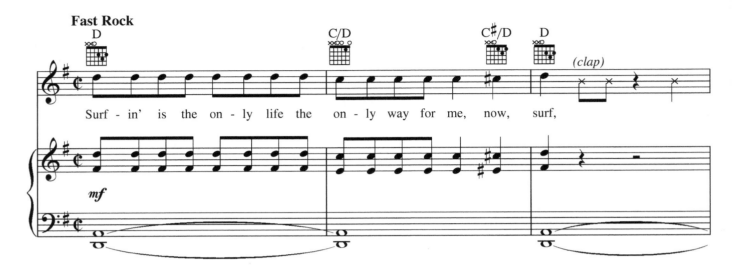

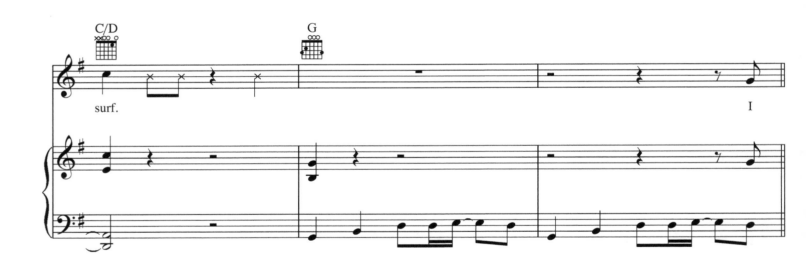

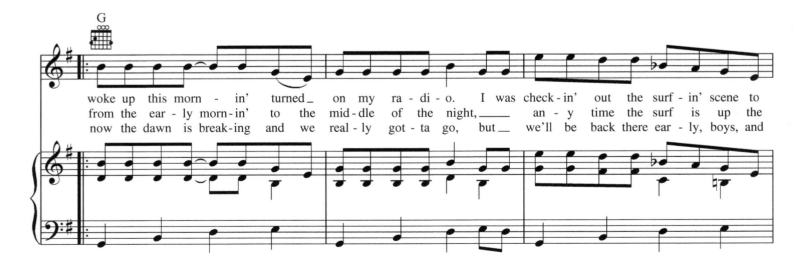

song 998973 job 32445 pvg kb

see if I would go, and when the dee - jay tells me that the surf is fine, that's
time ___ is right. And when the surf is down, ___ to take its place, we'll
that you bet - ter know. ___ Well, my surf-in' knots are ris - in' and my board is los - in' wax, but

when I know my babe and I will have a good ___ time. ___
do the surf - er stomp. ___ It's the lat - est dance ___ craze. ___
that won't stop me, ba - by, 'cause you know I'm com - in' back. ___

Surf - in', ___   surf - in', ___   surf - in', ___

surf - in', ___   surf - in', ___   surf - in', ___

SURFIN' SAFARI

Words and Music by BRIAN WILSON
and MIKE LOVE

Bright Rock

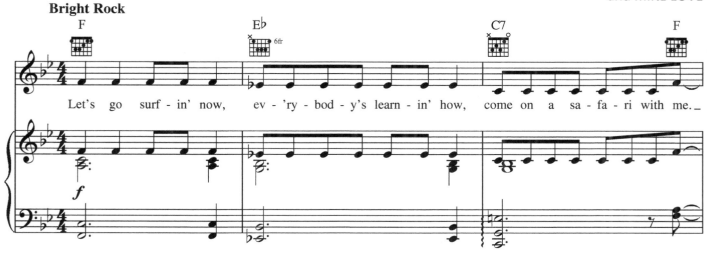

Let's go surf-in' now, ev-'ry-bod-y's learn-in' how, come on a sa-fa-ri with me.____

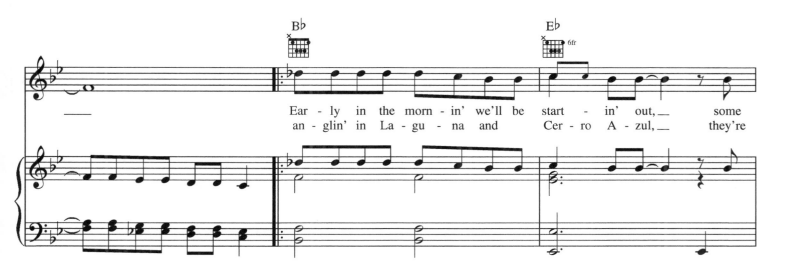

____ Ear-ly in the morn-in' we'll be start-in' out,____ some
an-glin' in La-gu-na and Cer-ro A-zul,____ they're

hon-eys will be com-in' a-long.____ We're load-in' up our wood-y with the
kick-in' out in Do-hi-ni too.____ I tell you surf-in's run-nin' wild, it's get-tin'

SURFIN' U.S.A.

Music by CHUCK BERRY
Words by BRIAN WILSON

THE WARMTH OF THE SUN

Words and Music by BRIAN WILSON
and MIKE LOVE

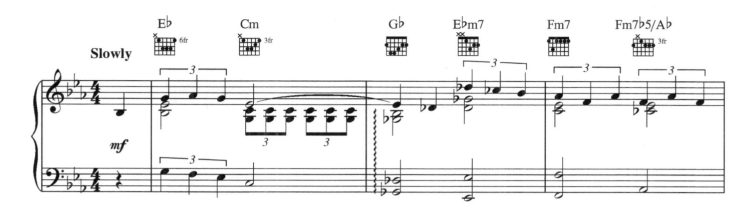

What good is the dawn _____ that grows in - to
love of my life, _____ she left me one

day? _____
day; _____

The sun - set at night _____
I cried when she said, _____

WENDY

Words and Music by BRIAN WILSON
and MIKE LOVE

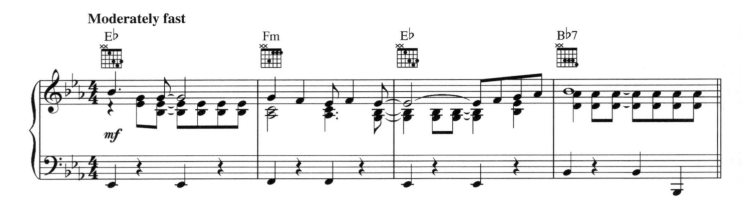

Wen - dy, ___ Wen - dy, what went wrong? ___ Oh so
Wen - dy, ___ Wen - dy don't lose your head, ___ lose your
Wen - dy, ___ I would - n't hurt you like that, ___ no, no,

wrong. We went ___ to - ge - ther for so long.
head. Wen - dy, ___ don't be - lieve a word he said. ___
no. I thought ___ we had our love down pat. ___

WHEN I GROW UP
(To Be a Man)

Words and Music by BRIAN WILSON
and MIKE LOVE

WILD HONEY

Words and Music by BRIAN WILSON
and MIKE LOVE

Bright Rock

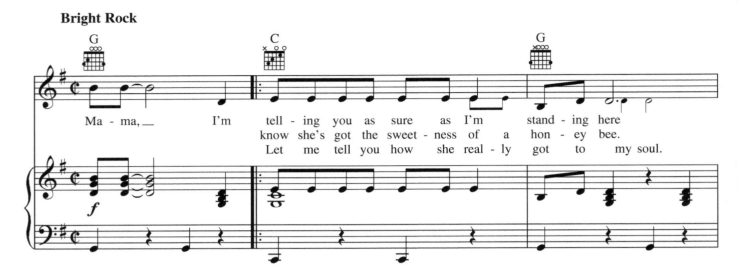

Ma - ma, __ I'm tell - ing you as sure as I'm stand - ing here
know she's got the sweet - ness of a hon - ey bee.
Let me tell you how she real - ly got to my soul.

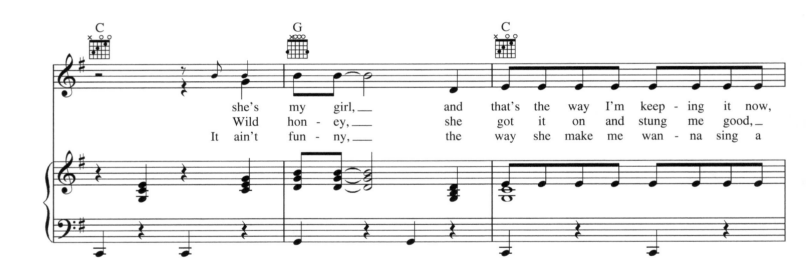

she's my girl, __ and that's the way I'm keep - ing it now,
Wild hon - ey, __ she got it on and stung me good, __
It ain't fun - ny, __ the way she make me wan - na sing a

ma - ma, dear.
yes - sir - ee.
lit - tle rock and roll.
No good will it do __ you to
With all the oth - er stud bees
There's noth - ing quite sweet __ as a

YOU'RE SO GOOD TO ME

Words and Music by BRIAN WILSON
and MIKE LOVE

YOUR SUMMER DREAM

Words and Music by BRIAN WILSON
and BOB NORBERG

WOULDN'T IT BE NICE

Words by and Music by BRIAN WILSON,
TONY ASHER and MIKE LOVE

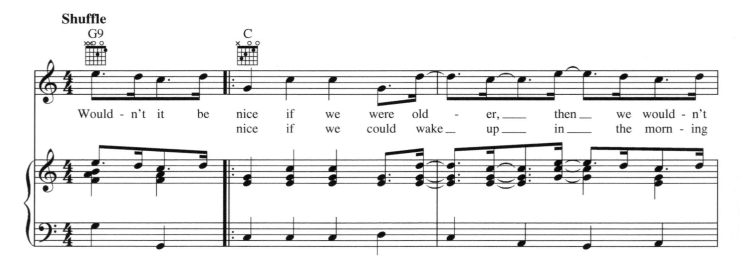